CHALLENGE

90 DAYS TO FULFILLING FAITH

Nathan Faught

THE CHALLENGE: 90 DAYS TO FULFILLING FAITH

Copyright © 2012 by Nathan D. Faught. All rights reserved

No portion of this book may be reproduced, stored in a retrieval system, or transmitted in any form or by any means – electronic, mechanical, photocopy, recording or any other – except for brief quotations in printed reviews, without the prior permission of the publisher.

Published in association with CreateSpace by Amazon.com

ISBN-13: 978-1478302834

ISBN-10: 1478302836

ACKNOWLEDGMENTS

The following people have made wonderful contributions to this project and I am sincerely humbled and grateful for their love and support.

First and foremost, the love of my life, my wife Amanda and our two amazing boys, Alex & Hayden, you all are my joy and my motivation. My world is a beautiful place because of our family.

Pastor Jonathan Suber – my friend, mentor and pastor. Thank you so much for believing in me and your amazing support!
www.TheSubers.tv

Steven Paul – thank you so much for your continued coaching and inspiration. You are an amazing friend.
www.churchpayroll.com

Carol Round – my editor and friend. Your hard work and dedication have left me speechless. You truly are an amazing author and Godly lady.
www.carolaround.com

My grandfather, Leo Faught – although our earthly time together was cut short in 1992 you have continued to be an amazing role model and my rock. You saw that God would do this through me long before I ever dreamed it could happen.

Finally, to my Lord and Savior, Jesus Christ, you are my source, my supply, my architect and friend. Everything I have and everything I am is yours.

FORWARD

I truly believe most everyone on earth wants to better themselves, but most of us have difficulty finding the right tools or resources. This is why I am so excited about the F-90 Challenge. Nathan Faught has found these tools for us and has broken them down to where anyone, on any level of their life mission can use them as an invaluable resource .

I believe in Nathan Faught. I have personally witnessed him as a living testimony of the concepts and insights he has mined out of the hard soil of life experience. He has an amazing family, a flourishing ministry and an amazing network of fellow pilgrims that he is helping along this quest of significance and success in our lives.

Anyone can make excuses, but it takes passion to accept a challenge! I encourage you to take 90 days and join the rest of us and change your life. If you do all that you can then God will do what He alone can do!

Jonathan Suber
Pastor, Speaker & Mentor
www.The Subers.tv

INTRODUCTION

This is not a devotional! This is a challenge!

FAITH! There is absolutely nothing in this world like it. When you have faith you feel on top of the world…ready to leap tall buildings in a single bound…ok, maybe not that extreme. However, this intangible, often illusive and difficult to define characteristic is without a doubt very powerful.

I do not know of a single person who would say that they don't need faith. In addition, not only do we all need faith, we all need to build our faith.

Faith is the single thing that God responds to. He does not respond to need. There are many people in great need that are not receiving from God. God does not respond to pain or desperation. There are thousands in pain and desperate for help that are not receiving from God. Time and time again throughout the Bible God very clearly states that he responds to FAITH.

What then is keeping your life from being full of God, full of His blessings and on fire with His purpose? If God responds to faith and you are in need of anything from Him what should you do?

Generate Faith
Manifest Faith
Build Faith
Establish Faith
Initiate Faith

Great! However, the million dollar question is not so much what you need as it is how you get it. I know that I need to generate, manifest, build, establish and initiate faith but how?

In Romans 12:3 Scripture lets us know that God has given to every human being a measure of faith. Therefore, whether you realize it or not, you actually already have faith. Think of faith as a muscle. You already have muscles. There is no need to create new ones. However, for the muscles in your body to grow and be able to do what they were meant to do they need three things. First, they need to be fed the proper nutrients. Second, they need to be exercised. Finally, they need proper rest.

Your faith is no different than the physical muscles in your body. In fact, I want you to think of faith as your spiritual muscle. If given the right nutrients, exercise and rest, not only will your faith grow but will become stronger and stronger having greater and greater impact in your life.

THE CHALLENGE

In the following pages God has inspired me to share with you 90 days of feeding, exercising and rejuvenating your faith! These daily challenges have three parts.

First, you will read a Power Thought designed to refresh your faith. Second, I share a daily scripture that will feed your faith from God's Word. Finally, there is a daily Faith Challenge, designed to exercise your faith.

Take each challenge one day at a time. Let me also encourage you not to skip over a challenge. There will be days that it doesn't feel like a particular challenge is applicable to what you are going through. However, just as you wouldn't go to the gym and only exercise the muscles you felt like working on, neither should you treat your faith muscles in this manner.

Finally know that you are not alone! I have seen so many wonderful individuals just like yourself take a faith challenge and are now living an extraordinary life!

You deserve this.
GO FOR IT!

#1
HARNESS YOUR MIND

What happens in your mind
is likely to happen in your future.
Today's thoughts become tomorrow's reality.
Meditate on specific Scriptures today that will unlock your
faith in God. Make your mind your servant. Fill your Mental
Warehouse with the Word of God!

***"Summing it all up, friends, I'd say you'll do best by filling
your minds and meditating on things true, noble, reputable,
authentic, compelling, gracious - the best, not the worst; the
beautiful, not the ugly; things to praise, not things to curse"
Philippians 4:8 (The Message).***

FAITH CHALLENGE:
Take 90 seconds and write the above scripture on an index
card or paper that you can keep in front of you all day! Read it
every time you feel your mind wandering!

NOTES:_____

_____

_____

_____

_____

_____

#2
TWO EARS ONE MOUTH

Do you really listen? Somebody knows something you don't. That information may be invaluable. You have to listen to receive it. Something inside you may want to scream out for attention. You have a longing to be heard. Restrain yourself and learn to listen before you speak. How often does God speak? As often as you are willing to listen!

"...let the wise listen and add to their learning, and let the discerning get guidance"
Proverbs 1:5 (NIV).

FAITH CHALLENGE:
Take 90 seconds and practice listening. Ask God to teach you to hear the voice of the Holy Spirit. It is the single most valuable voice in the life of mankind!

NOTES:

#3
CONNECT WITH A MENTOR

Warfare is the ideal time
to connect with your mentor(s).
Consult the mentor most likely to build your faith.
Moses was a mentor to Joshua.
Paul was a mentor to Timothy.
Elijah was a mentor to Elisha.
Your mentor is the bridge to your victory!

"It's better to be wise than strong; intelligence outranks muscle any day. Strategic planning is the key to warfare; to win, you need a lot of good counsel"
Proverbs 24:5-6 (The Message).

FAITH CHALLENGE:
Take 90 seconds and call, email or text a mentor and ask to spend some time with him/her this week. Even if it is over the phone or through email, connect with someone who will build and challenge your faith.

NOTES:_____

#4
BE TENACIOUS

Life is a collection of battles and victories to be won Consequently, it is also the home field for champions. Reach deep inside and grab hold of your greatest strength. Today is not a day for weakness. It is a time to be tenacious!

*"A wise man has great power,
and a man of knowledge increases strength"
Proverbs 24:5 (NIV).*

*"Finally, be strong in the Lord and in his mighty power"
Ephesians 6:10 (NIV).*

FAITH CHALLENGE:
Take 90 seconds and write down three of your strengths! Keep these three where you can see them all day and maximize your focus for victory!

NOTES:

1) I love People + work well with others.
2) I'm smart + knowledgeable
3) I'm a good speaker + teacher

#5
SEE THE BIG PICTURE

Nothing is ever as it first appears!
Pain passes. Adversity passes.
Look beyond your current hardships.
Something incredible is coming your way!
The resurrection followed the crucifixion.
Promotion follows adversity.
So, get your eyes on the bigger picture.

"These hard times are small potatoes compared to the coming good times, the lavish celebration prepared for us"
II Corinthians 4:17 (The Message).

FAITH CHALLENGE:
Take 90 seconds and ask God to show you the bigger picture and give you strength to succeed in adversity!

NOTES:_____

_____

_____

_____

_____

_____

_____

_____

#6
GIVE GOD TIME

Jesus invested His first 30 years in preparation for His ministry. Moses spent 80 years becoming a great leader. Time is your friend, don't hurry. Remember, patience is the weapon that forces deception to reveal itself.

"God proves to be good to the man who passionately waits, to the woman who diligently seeks. It's a good thing to quietly hope, quietly hope for help from God"
Lamentations 3:25-26 (The Message).

FAITH CHALLENGE:
Take 90 seconds and be quiet. It is easy to be anxious. When these times come train yourself to "reset" by patiently waiting on God.

NOTES:

#7
GET TO KNOW GOD'S VOICE

The greatest success you will ever accomplish is learning the voice of God. As His child, every blessing comes from an instruction. To receive the instruction, you must learn His voice. God talks often. You will have to spend time with Him often to know His voice.

"My sheep recognize my voice.
I know them, and they follow me"
John 10:27 (The Message).

FAITH CHALLENGE:
Take 90 seconds during your prayer time and be quiet! As long as you are talking God will not. However, once you begin to hear Him talk you will learn that He talks often to those who are willing to learn His voice.

NOTES:

#8
GET THE MESSAGE

When Satan wants to destroy you, he sends a person into your life. When God wants to bless you, he sends a person into your life. Recognize them! Whether they are packaged as someone with great stature and prestige or none at all, your reaction to a man or woman of God is carefully documented by God. When God talks to you, it is often through the spiritual leaders in your life.

"Accepting a messenger of God is as good as being God's messenger. Accepting someone's help is as good as giving someone help"
Matthew 10:41 (The Message).

FAITH CHALLENGE:
Take 90 seconds and ask God to show you the messengers that He has sent into your life. You must also ask Him to make you sensitive that you may receive the message.

NOTES:

#9
OBEDIENCE IS THE SEED FOR MIRACLES

You have listened to and obeyed the instruction of God. Now, expect the miraculous! Blessings are benefits from God that increase your joy and enable you to fulfill His purpose in your life. However, blessings are promised only to the obedient. Obedience is always rewarded.
Obedience is proof of your faith in God.

"All these blessings will come upon you and accompany you if you obey the LORD your God"
Deuteronomy 28:2 (NIV).

"No good thing will He withhold from those who walk uprightly"
Psalms 84:11 (NKJV).

FAITH CHALLENGE:
Take 90 seconds and write down three things that you can do this week in obedience to God's instructions.

NOTES:

1) Finish School w/ excellence
2) Accept the Pastor Position.
3) Continue to walk in purity

#10
GOD'S SCHEDULE

Your schedule for today should be decided in the presence of God. Your daily agenda will create miracles or tragedies, depending on whether or not you are led by the Spirit of God. Your inner peace is a signal. Don't make a phone call, an appointment or a decision unless you are at peace in your heart about it. Live with God's schedule.

"...for those who are led by the Spirit of God are the children of God"
Romans 8:14 (NIV).

FAITH CHALLENGE:
Take 90 seconds and evaluate your schedule. Ask God to give you peace about those things that line up with His schedule and remove those things that do not.

NOTES:

#11
ASK & KEEP ASKING

Someone knows something you need to know. Something that can help you succeed and grow in this, the most important chapter of your life. Ignorance is deadly. Don't risk it.
If you don't know who to ask, ask God.
True champions do.

***"Without good direction, people lose their way; the more wise counsel you follow,
the better your chances"
Proverbs 11:14 (The Message).***

FAITH CHALLENGE:
Take 90 seconds and write down three things that you need to know about to succeed in this chapter in your life. Now, beside each of these write down the name of someone with whom you can connect to help you learn.
If you don't know anyone, then ask God.

NOTES:_____

_____

_____

_____

_____

#12
ANALYZE ADVERSITY

There are four ways to respond to crisis:
Maximize it... Minimize it... Advertise it... Analyze it.
Maximizing is to exaggerate the crisis. Minimizing is to ignore the crisis. Advertising is to tell the whole world about it. Analyzing is extracting useful information from it. Crisis is merely concentrated information. Adversity is your enemies' reaction to your progress.

"On a good day, enjoy yourself;
On a bad day, examine..."
Ecclesiastes 7:14 (The Message).

FAITH CHALLENGE:
Take 90 seconds and evaluate your adversity. What can you learn? What information is there that you can use? There is something valuable that God will reveal,
if you will seek His counsel.

NOTES:

#13
THE BENEFITS OF ENDURANCE

Every situation is for a reason. Every circumstance is for a season. Don't eject…endure! Endurance is always rewarded. When you are tired, exhausted and discouraged don't quit. Get alone with God and endure.
It is the one thing in eternity that will be rewarded

"He who stands firm to the end will be saved"
Matthew 10:22 (NIV).

"Don't quit. Don't cave in.
It is all well worth it in the end"
Matthew 10:22 (The Message).

FAITH CHALLENGE:
Take 90 seconds and ask God to teach you the weapon of endurance. Your enemy will lose, not you, if you allow God to teach you endurance.

NOTES:_____

#14
REMEMBER SEASONS CHANGE

Attacks don't last forever.
Bad days don't last forever.
People change. The weather changes. Circumstances change.
So don't be discouraged today. Tomorrow is coming.
Your future is bright...God says so!
Your future is unlike any yesterday
you have ever known.

*"The nights of crying your eyes out give way
to days of laughter"
Psalms 30:5 (The Message).*

FAITH CHALLENGE:
Take 90 seconds to look at the big picture. Push back from those things that seem to be pressing so hard against you.
Listen to God's voice during this season.
He is preparing you for a bright tomorrow.

NOTES:

#15
READ THE STORIES OF CHAMPIONS

Everyone is different. Some people are winners and some are losers. A few are champions.
Consider the Biblical accounts of Joshua, David, Abraham and the Apostle Paul. Visit your local library, invest in a Kindle or iPad and begin reading the biographies of great men and women. Every highly successful winner has learned the power of a champion's story.

"Keep your eyes on Jesus, who both began and finished this race we're in. Study how he did it "
Hebrews 12:2 (The Message)

FAITH CHALLENGE:
Take 90 seconds and write down the names of three people who inspire you. Find at least one book and begin studying these champions this week.

NOTES:_____

_____

_____

_____

_____

_____

_____

#16
DON'T SPEAK GRASSHOPPER

Moses sent 12 men to spy on the land of Canaan. Ten of the spies came back speaking defeat. "We're nothing. We are like grasshoppers next to those huge giants." However, the remaining two were giant killers. Joshua and Caleb refused to speak grasshopper. Instead they declared, "We are well able to overcome the giants." God gave them the land and they defeated every giant they faced!

"And they spread among the Israelites a bad report about the land they had explored...We saw the Nephilim there. We seemed like grasshoppers in our own eyes, and we looked the same to them"
Numbers 13:32-33 (NIV).

FAITH CHALLENGE:
Take 90 seconds and ask God to remove all grasshopper talk from your vocabulary. Refuse to speak defeat!

NOTES:

#17
KNOW YOUR EXPERTISE

Highly successful people know what they are good at and leverage it. Even in your mother's womb you were given special gifts, talents and abilities. What you enjoy doing the most is a clue to what God wants you to do with your life. Trying to live outside of your expertise will only build frustration. Stick with what you're good at.

"Let every man abide in the same calling wherein he was called"
I Corinthians 7:20 (KJV).

FAITH CHALLENGE:
Take 90 seconds and write down three things that you know you are good at or that you enjoy doing the most. Now look at your agenda for the week and find ways to leverage your expertise in those areas each day.

NOTES:

1) Teaching others
2) Playing music
3) Reaching out to my peers

#18
THINK AHEAD

I call it "The Guaranteed Future." If you eat two slices of chocolate cake every night, what is the guaranteed outcome? If you smoke two packs of cigarettes a day, what is the guaranteed outcome? Whatever you are doing right now is producing an inevitable future! You must train yourself to see your future by what you are doing today.

"Do not be deceived: God cannot be mocked.
A man reaps what he sows"
Galatians 6:7 (NIV).

FAITH CHALLENGE:
Take 90 seconds and forecast your future by what you are doing right now. Then, decide the future you want and begin to live toward that future.
Think ahead!

NOTES:

#19
KEEP WALKING

Picture this; you are driving through a rainstorm. Although it is difficult to see, you don't stop. You keep driving. Why? Because you know you will eventually move out of the storm. Remember Joseph. Remember David. Every day of adversity is simply one step closer to your victory.
Keep walking!

"When you're in over your head, I'll be there with you. When you're in rough waters, you will not go down....Because I am God, your personal God...your Savior. I paid a huge price for you"
Isaiah 43:2-3 (The Message).

FAITH CHALLENGE:
Take 90 seconds and ask God to help you keep walking knowing you are closer and closer to victory!

NOTES:_____

#20
DO WHAT YOU LOVE

Whatever brings you the most fulfillment is an important key to your life. God wants you happy. That is a settled issue. Now find what makes you happy. You will have extraordinary success with something that becomes your obsession.

"So I saw that there is nothing better for a man than to enjoy his work, because that is his lot"
Ecclesiastes 3:22 (NIV).

FAITH CHALLENGE:
Take 90 seconds and write down three things that you love to do. Allow yourself some time this week to brainstorm ideas on how you could use what you love and what your good at to bring fulfillment.

NOTES:

#21
BE CREATIVE IN A TEST

A test is your moment to shine. Problems are opportunities for you to show off your skills, talents and abilities. Use challenges as laboratories to create new solutions. Can God trust you with trouble? Champions are made in the heat of battle not in the locker room.

"Anyone who meets a testing challenge head-on and manages to stick it out is mighty fortunate. For such persons loyally in love with God, the reward is life and more life"
James 1:12 (The Message).

FAITH CHALLENGE:
Take 90 seconds and choose to see the challenges in front of you in a different light. Take some time today to brainstorm new, creative solutions.

NOTES:_____

#22
LOOK FOR DOUBLE BLESSING

Read carefully the stories of Job, Joseph and Daniel. Their adversity always birthed a season of Double Blessing in their lives. They discovered that false accusation is often the last stage before supernatural promotion. Miracles are coming your way. Recognize them and look for a Double Blessing today!

"After Job had interceded for his friends, God restored his fortune - and then doubled it!"
Job 42:10 (The Message).

FAITH CHALLENGE:
Take 90 seconds and ask God to help you come into alignment with what He wants for your life. Seek the blesser not the blessing, the healer not the healing, the deliverer not the deliverance.

NOTES:

#23
ASK, ASK, ASK

Everything comes from someone. Whatever you need already exists. Ask with joy. Ask with expectation. Ask with gratitude. You can never ask and be worse off. You can hear "no" which means nothing has changed. So what do you have to lose? Someone, somewhere, is willing to help you,
but you have to ask!

"...you do not have because you do not ask"
James 4:2 (NKJV).

FAITH CHALLENGE:
Take 90 seconds and decide what it is that you need and who you could ask assistance from. Picture yourself receiving with joy, expectation and gratitude.
Now ask with that vision in mind!

NOTES:

#24
DON'T RUSH IT

Great things take time! Human pregnancy takes
nine months. Jesus took 30 years to prepare for His earthly
ministry. You must willingly pace yourself
on this journey to success. Your present and future joy
depends on it. Hurrying is a huge risk for regret.

*"A man with an evil eye hastens after riches, and does not
consider that poverty will come upon him"*
Proverbs 28:22 (NKJV).

FAITH CHALLENGE:
Take 90 seconds and ask God to help you slow down.
Meditating on the things of God and His purposes for your life
is a great way to bring calmness and perspective
to what could be a hasty mistake.

NOTES:

#25
CREDIT YOUR REAL SOURCE

Everything you have God gave you. Never forget it.
Don't let any success go to your head. It is too easy to pat
ourselves on the back for the 10 percent we give,
when God gave the 100 percent we have.
He is your complete source.
Champions always credit the real source.

"But remember the LORD your God, for it is he who gives you the ability to produce wealth, and so confirms his covenant" Deuteronomy 8:18 (NIV).

FAITH CHALLENGE:
Take 90 seconds and give God glory for the things He has done;
for the job that He gives you the ability to handle, for the health
He gives you to enjoy, for the success
He allows you to accomplish.

NOTES:

#26
MANAGE EACH DAY

Time is extremely valuable. It is the currency of life. When you are wasting your time, you are wasting your life. Managing your time wisely is one of the most important keys to success. Keep a written list of your daily tasks. Invest in time management applications for your computer or mobile device. The accurate arrangement of things is the power key to productivity.

"...redeeming the time, because the days are evil"
Ephesians 5:16 (NKJV).

FAITH CHALLENGE:
Take 90 seconds at the beginning of each day to create a "To-Do" list. If you own a smart phone, make use of the calendar reminders and applications to help you manage your time and tasks.

NOTES:

#27
CREATE EFFECTIVE DECISIONS

Your life hinges on the decisions you make. Your decisions will lead to tragedy or joy, laughter or tears, pain or pleasure. Don't let anyone rush you into any decision before you are prepared. At the same time, you cannot allow yourself to be paralyzed by too much analysis.

Champions are both prepared and courageous in making effective decisions.

" Lead with your ears, follow up with your tongue, and let anger straggle along in the rear"
James 1:19 (The Message).

FAITH CHALLENGE:
Take 90 seconds and write down Proverbs 3:5-6 and implement these verses into your prayer time. Ask God for wisdom and guidance in all decisions.

NOTES:

#28
NEVER, NEVER, NEVER GIVE UP

Your dreams and goals are worth any fight,
any waiting, any price. Don't give up.
Your perseverance demoralizes your enemy.
Don't give up. Patience is a weapon.
Don't give up!

"Jesus replied, 'No one who puts his hand to the plow and looks back is fit for service in the kingdom of God'"
Luke 9:62 (NIV).

FAITH CHALLENGE:
Take 90 seconds and ask for help. When we are at a low point (stressed, tired, vulnerable, etc.) our enemy goes for the kill. Too many people give up without ever asking for help. Reach out to someone today and never, never, never give up!

NOTES:

#29
REMEMBER THE POOR

Thousands are homeless, destitute and impoverished. Your reaction to them determines God's reaction to you. Get involved. Plant your best seed into a church or worthy organization committed to helping those who are less fortunate. Your own prosperity will be affected by it

"Mercy to the needy is a loan to God, and God pays back those loans in full"
Proverbs 19:17 (The Message).

FAITH CHALLENGE:
Take 90 seconds and find a church or organization in your area with which you can volunteer. Sometimes it is just too easy to send money. Regardless of how you do it,
make it a point to remember the poor.

NOTES:_____

#30
THE LITTLE THINGS

Little hinges swing big doors. Acorns produce oak trees. Little things really do matter. Develop a passion for details. Don't forget the basics: keep a budget, write a to-do list, pay your bills, arrive to work on time, and plant your seeds
Into the Kingdom of God.

"'Well done, good and faithful servant! You have been faithful with a few things; I will put you in charge of many things. Come and share your master's happiness!'"
Matthew 25:23 (NIV).

FAITH CHALLENGE:
Take 90 seconds and refocus on the day in front of you. Busy seasons are an easy time to lose focus on the daily details that will bring both short term and long-term success.

NOTES:

#31
FAITH SIGNS

What you see determines what you feel. So put faith signs on your refrigerator, bathroom mirror and desk that inspire you. Change your thoughts and you can change your world. Your faith signs will remind you to think life-changing thoughts.

"'Mine eye affecteth mine heart"
Lamentations 3:51 (KJV).

FAITH CHALLENGE:
Take 90 seconds and grab some sticky notes. Now write down some phrases, quotes or scriptures that inspire you. Put them in everyday places where you will see them: on your desk, bathroom mirror, car dashboard, refrigerator, inside your wallet, etc.

NOTES:

#32
JOY TO THE WORLD

Joy is the result of consistently spending time with Jesus, talking to Him, thinking on Him and reading his word. This relationship with Christ has been over-complicated by religion. It is as simple as any human friendship one might have, yet, it is more powerful than any human can offer.

"You will fill me with joy in your presence, with eternal pleasures at your right hand"
Psalms 16:11 (NIV).

FAITH CHALLENGE:
Take 90 seconds and talk to Jesus as if He were sitting across the kitchen table from you. Share with Him your dreams and fears; pour your heart out to Him. As you do this, you will feel His presence. As with any relationship, the more you do this, the more you will draw closer to Him.

NOTES:

#33
READ...LISTEN...OBSERVE

The difference between today and your future is information. If you don't learn anything new today, tomorrow will be no different. This means that you don't have a future, just a longer today.
Therefore, you must read...listen...observe.
Your future is in your discoveries.

"Without good direction, people lose their way; the more wise counsel you follow, the better your chances"
Proverbs 11:14 (The Message).

FAITH CHALLENGE:
Take 90 seconds and make a list of books you can read, magazines you can subscribe to and people you can meet with that will allow you to better your chances of success. Now commit to using these resources on a weekly basis by scheduling time in your calendar.

NOTES:

1) Leadership & Pastoral help books.
2) Re read books from WBF
3) Pastor Fred & Pastor Jon
4) Motivational Podcasts

#34
DOUBT PRODUCES TRAGEDIES

Some words grieve the heart of God. Some words excite His heart. Unbelief brings God pain. Faith brings Him great pleasure. Twelve spies analyzed Canaan for 40 days. Moses and the people accepted the Report of Doubt from the 10 spies instead of the Report of Faith from Joshua and Caleb. Each day of doubt brought 365 days of heartache (Numbers 14:34).
Doubt is as contagious as faith!

"And without faith it is impossible to please God"
Hebrews 11:6 (NIV).

FAITH CHALLENGE:
Take 90 seconds and make a commitment to God and yourself that when the Report of Doubt comes you will instead choose to please Him with your Report of Faith.

NOTES:

#35
SCREEN DOUBTERS

Screen doors prevent obnoxious insects from entering your home. You must assertively screen out people who are carriers of the virus of Doubt and Unbelief. Boldly protect your ears and life from absorbing talk that does not edify and build.

Jesus did it, you should too:
"Jesus didn't swerve. 'Peter, get out of my way. Satan, get lost. You have no idea how God works.'"
Matthew 16:23 (The Message).

FAITH CHALLENGE:
Take 90 seconds and make a commitment to God and yourself that when people around you began to speak doubt and unbelief that you will walk away
from that conversation immediately.

NOTES:_____

_____

_____

_____

_____

_____

_____

#36
GREAT RESEARCH=GREAT DECISIONS

Your life is the result of the decisions that you have made. Your decisions can create success, peace and joy. They can also create poverty, frustration and negativity. Do not let anyone or anything rush you into a decision before you have had time to prepare. Be patient.
Thorough research creates effective decisions!

"My dear brothers, take note of this: Everyone should be quick to listen, slow to speak and slow to become angry…"
James 1:19 (NIV).

FAITH CHALLENGE:
Take 90 seconds, slow down and make a plan for research. Those things that you are facing right now can wait for you to gather more information. Then, when you have great information don't hesitate to make a great decision.

NOTES:

#37
NETWORK WITH OTHERS

Note: you cannot multiply by using the number 1.
Develop people skills. Listen, learn and absorb from others.
Ask questions and document answers.
Success is a collection of relationships.
Whatever you are willing to settle for determines
the quality of your future

"It's better to have a partner than go it alone. Share the work, share the wealth. And if one falls down, the other helps, But if there's no one to help, tough!"
Ecclesiastes 4:9-10 (The Message).

FAITH CHALLENGE:
Take 90 seconds to evaluate the relationships you have. Are these relationships capable of multiplying you? If so, build on them. If not, reconsider why you have
that particular relationship.

NOTES:_____

_____

_____

_____

_____

_____

_____

#38
DESIGN A DETAILED PLAN

Your vision is your future. The Bible is God's written list of goals. He wrote down what He wanted to happen. It may be difficult for you to transfer your thoughts, but do it. Something wonderful starts happening when you actually see a blueprint of your future.

"Write the vision and make it plain on tablets, that he may run who reads it"
Habakkuk 2:2 (NKJV).

FAITH CHALLENGE:
Take 90 seconds and start a journal of your thoughts, ideas, dreams and goals. You can even do this electronically as there are many applications and online resources at your fingertips.

NOTES:

#39
BE DILIGENT

Diligence is speedy attention to an assigned task. Respond immediately to instructions. Don't wait, act! According to the Bible this is a key element to promotion. So, move and move quickly...don't hesitate or procrastinate.
Move quickly and thoroughly to the tasks set before you

***"Lazy hands make a man poor,
but diligent hands bring wealth"
Proverbs 10:4 (NIV).***

FAITH CHALLENGE:
Take 90 seconds and review your "to-do" list. Are there tasks that have been transferred from previous days or omitted due to lack of desire? Make these a priority. Be known as the one who is able to tackle any and all projects with diligence and watch promotion pursue you.

NOTES:_____

_____

_____

_____

_____

_____

_____

#40
PURSUE GODLY WISDOM

Wisdom is doing what God would do in any given situation. Jesus is to us, the wisdom of God. Whatever you are facing, pursue what you know Jesus would do. However, also know that what Jesus would do can often go against conventional intellect. Godly wisdom is the Master Key for success.

"Sell everything and buy Wisdom! Forage for Understanding! Don't forget one word! Don't deviate an inch!"
Proverbs 4:5 (The Message).

FAITH CHALLENGE:
Take 90 seconds and ask God to give you His wisdom. Commit to yourself and to Him that you will begin to face every decision with seeking Him for what He would have you do - His knowledge, His understanding.

NOTES:

#41
TOO MUCH IS TOO COSTLY

Don't attempt too many things. A famous billionaire once said, "I've seen as many people fail from attempting too many things as I have from attempting too few." Don't overload yourself. It will break your focus. One of the main reasons people fail is broken focus. Find something worthy of consuming you, and pour your life into it!

"A double minded man is unstable in all his ways"
James 1:8 (KJV).

FAITH CHALLENGE:
Take 90 seconds and evaluate your "To-Do" list. Are there things that you are attempting that are robbing you of valuable energy & focus? Can these items be eliminated or delegated? Never be afraid to say, "NO" to tasks that take you off focus and off purpose.

NOTES:_____

_____

_____

_____

_____

_____

#42
LOOK FOR A PROBLEM TO SOLVE

Everything God created is a solution to a problem. Your worth and significance are determined by the kinds of problems you solve. If you want to earn $100 an hour, you must find a $100 an hour problem to solve. Your significance is not your similarity to others but your difference. Take what makes you different and solve a problem with it.

"Never walk away from someone who deserves help; your hand is God's hand for that person"
Proverbs 3:27 (The Message).

FAITH CHALLENGE:
Take 90 seconds and evaluate your differences. What problems can you solve with your unique set of talents and abilities?

NOTES:

#43
DON'T UNDERMINE YESTERDAY'S PRAYER

Let's imagine you have just asked God for the salvation of someone you love very much. He heard you. It matters to Him. His Word promises His response. Events are now in motion. Do not come back today and speak words of doubt and unbelief to God and others. You may paralyze everything God is doing.

"But when he asks, he must believe and not doubt, because he who doubts is like a wave of the sea, blown and tossed by the wind."
James 1:6 (NIV)

FAITH CHALLENGE:
Take 90 seconds and speak faith over the things that you have been asking God for. Find a scripture that inspires you and commit it to memory.

NOTES:

#44
RESPECT WORDS

When God wanted to create the World, He spoke. Words are creative forces that bring into existence that which has never before existed. Your words are some of the greatest gifts God has placed at your command. Use them wisely and you will discover one of the Golden Keys to Life.

"A small rudder on a huge ship in the hands of a skilled captain sets a course in the face of the strongest winds. A word out of your mouth may seem of no account, but it can accomplish nearly anything - or destroy it!"
James 3:4-5 (The Message).

FAITH CHALLENGE:
Take 90 seconds and ask God to help you be especially careful with your words.

NOTES:

#45
EVERY BATTLE IS A BRIDGE

David, with a simple slingshot, killed Goliath and eventually became king. Joseph endured the hatred of his brothers, false accusations and became second in power to Pharaoh. Study the battles of such champions and how they formed those battles to be bridges of destiny!

"...but the people who know their God shall be strong, and carry out great exploits!"
Daniel 11:32 (NKJV).

FAITH CHALLENGE:
Take 90 seconds and ask God to help you turn current battles into bridges. The enemy is only fighting you because there is a worth in you that he cannot stand.

NOTES:

#46
TALK EXPECTATIONS NOT EXPERIENCES

Do not drag yesterday into your future. Perhaps you have just been through a tough time. Do not concentrate on negative feelings. Instead point out the possibility of promotion, freedom and victory. Nurture the "Photograph of Possibilities." Elijah gave the widow of Zarephath a picture of her potential and it stirred the expectation of a miracle.

"Let us not become weary in doing good, for at the proper time we will reap a harvest if we do not give up"
Galatians 6:9 (NIV).

FAITH CHALLENGE:
Take 90 seconds and write down 5 expectations that you feel God would bring about in your life. Now ask God to help you let go of past experiences and speak in faith these expectations.

NOTES:

#47
RADIATE THANKFULNESS

Gratitude produces joy. It does not take a genius to discern and detect flaws. However, it takes great awareness to see the good things in life. Take time to appreciate God's "everyday-blessings." Breath, sight, hearing, clothes, food, shelter...and thousands of other things to be joyful about.

"This day is sacred to our Lord. Do not grieve, for the joy of the LORD is your strength"
Nehemiah 8:10 (NIV).

FAITH CHALLENGE:
Take 90 seconds and see how many things you can write down for which you are thankful. Don't stop; keep going. The more you name the better you'll feel, and the better you feel the more you will find to name.

NOTES:

#48
TALK GOD'S LANGUAGE

Your words affect God. Your prayers ignite God. Jesus taught His disciples how to talk to God about provision, protection and pardon. Faith-talk is what God responds to favorably. Confess your sins, your desire for forgiveness, and the things you need God to do in your life.

"...my God-defined people, respond by humbling themselves, praying, seeking my presence, and turning their backs on their wicked lives, I'll be there ready for you: I'll listen from heaven, forgive their sins, and restore their land to health"
II Chronicles 7:14 (The Message).

FAITH CHALLENGE:
Take 90 seconds and ask God to fill your words with His Spirit, His Anointing, and His Heart.

NOTES:_____

#49
MAKE TODAY AN EVENT

Do not be passive today. You are alive, act like it.
Talk like it. Celebrate. Speak a little louder today.
Smile bigger and laugh out loud!
Exude the joy of Jesus as you spread it lavishly over every aspect of your life and those around you.

*"This is the day the LORD has made;
let us rejoice and be glad in it"
Psalms 118:24 (NIV).*

FAITH CHALLENGE:
Take 90 seconds and take a deep breath. Rejoice. Smile. Laugh. Cheer. Applaud. Do something to put a smile on your face and on the face of someone near you.
CELEBRATE!

NOTES:

#50
STUDY PRAYER CHAMPIONS

Heroes are worth observing. The Bible is a Book of Champions. Read it carefully and you will see a parade of extraordinary people who changed the course of history through their prayer life. David, Daniel, Esther, Moses and Elijah are only a few of the thousands of Champions found in the Bible. Study their lives and learn.

"Elijah was a man just like us. He prayed earnestly that it would not rain, and it did not rain on the land for three and a half years"
James 5:17 (NIV).

FAITH CHALLENGE:
Take 90 seconds, choose one Bible character and make a commitment this week to study the way he or she prayed.

NOTES:_____

#51
MAKE LITTLE BLESSINGS GREAT CELEBRATIONS

Gorgeous sunsets. The laughter of children. Hot bubble baths.
A vacant parking space near the store.
Turn little blessings into a celebration. Life is a journey. Focus on the little things that make it enjoyable. You have already received, and received, and received so much from God. It is time to make much of what He has done.

"Sing praises over everything, any excuse for a song to God the Father in the name of our Master, Jesus Christ"
Ephesians 5:20 (The Message).

FAITH CHALLENGE:
Take 90 seconds and make a list of little blessings you can celebrate. See how many you can list in 90 seconds. GO!

NOTES:

#52
TALK ABOUT WHAT YOU LOVE

Enthusiasm breeds excitement. Enthusiasm is the only climate in which "Seeds of Success" will grow. If you want others to get involved in your dreams, you must exude an attitude of excitement. Your energy will attract others to your dream.

*"Words kill, words give life;
they're either poison or fruit - you choose"
Proverbs 18:21 (The Message).*

FAITH CHALLENGE:
Take 90 seconds and write down the names of three people who you will have a discussion with today about your dreams. Now commit to engage those three conversations with enthusiasm and excitement.

NOTES:

1) Chuell Paxton
2) John McIntosh
3) Amanda

#53
SAVOR THE MOMENT

Savor means to taste, feel and extract all the pleasure and benefit of each moment. Someone once said, "You are going to be on the journey longer than you will be at the destination...so enjoy the journey! Always BE where you are at. Don't permit your mind to race miles ahead of where your body is. Taste "NOW." It is the future you were talking about yesterday.

*"Behold, now is the accepted time; behold,
now is the day of salvation"
II Corinthians 6:2 (NKJV).*

FAITH CHALLENGE:
Take 90 seconds and see how many things you can write down about what you are experiencing right now. Extract all the pleasure and benefit of this moment.

NOTES:

#54
ASK BETTER QUESTIONS

Stop asking yourself questions that do not have answers, such as, "Why did this happen to me?" "Why do they treat me this way?" Ask yourself creative questions such as, "What can I do right now to create change?" "How can I improve this situation?" Your mind will work to produce answers to every question you ask it. So, don't exhaust it.
Ask better questions.

"Ask and it will be given to you; seek and you will find; knock and the door will be opened to you"
Matthew 7:7 (NIV).

FAITH CHALLENGE:
Take 90 seconds and these two questions:
What can I do right now to create change?
How can I improve this situation?

NOTES:

#55
SOAK UP GOD'S PROMISES

Study the covenant that God establishes with those who walk in obedience to Him. You can only operate in faith according to your knowledge of His will & desire for your life. If you don't know that God has already provided for your healing, how can you believe Him for a miracle in your health? You must have a photograph of the will of God so your faith can develop it.

"...for he who comes to God must believe that He is, and that He is a rewarder of those who diligently seek Him" Hebrews 11:6 (NKJV).

FAITH CHALLENGE:
Take 90 seconds and ask God to lead you to the promises in His Word. Now commit to spending time researching those promises and developing your faith in Him.

NOTES:

#56
INSPIRE OTHERS TO GET INVOLVED

What you lack is always housed in someone else. God never intended you to succeed alone. When you pray today, ask God to direct you to someone He has chosen to partner with you. Reaching toward others takes humility.
The willingness to ask is proof of your passion.
Inspire others to get involved in your dreams.

"Ask and it will be given to you; seek and you will find; knock and the door will be opened to you"
Matthew 7:7 (NIV).

FAITH CHALLENGE:
Take 90 seconds and ask God to lead you to three people who you can inspire. Ask Him to place in their hearts what He is placing in your heart.

NOTES:

#57
GO GO GO

God never intended the church to be salt warehouses. He designed us to be salt-shakers. You were meant to bring flavor to the lives of those around you. The Body of Christ (the Church) and the Gospel Message are the spice of life.
You don't bring the food to the salt,
you take the salt to the food.

*" You're here to be salt-seasoning that brings out the God-flavors of this earth. If you lose your saltiness,
how will people taste godliness?"
Matthew 5:13 (The Message).*

FAITH CHALLENGE:
Take 90 seconds and visit
www.GoBeChrist.com
and partner with us to be salt shakers.

NOTES:

#58
DON'T FORGET PAST VICTORIES

Think about your past battles and struggles. David remembered and replayed the victory over the bear and the lion before he ran toward Goliath. Yesterday is your history of success. Remember them and talk about them. Satan is the only one you will irritate.

"In the future, when your children ask you, 'What do these stones mean?' These stones are to be a memorial to the people of Israel forever"
Joshua 4:6-7 (NIV).

FAITH CHALLENGE:
Take 90 seconds and write down three past victories that come to mind. Now keep these in front of you all day long and let them inspire you to more victory.

NOTES:

1) helping to get children save last year.
2) Ministering in the prison
3) Overcoming lust

#59
SEEING IS INSPIRATIONAL

What you see determines how you feel. So, put photos and pictures around your house, office, desk and even your car that inspire your faith. God instructed the children of Israel to put His Word as signs before their eyes on the doorposts of their homes (Deuteronomy 11:18-25).

"Mine eye affecteth mine heart"
Lamentations 3:51 (KJV).

FAITH CHALLENGE:
Take 90 seconds and design a plan for placing inspirational images in your life. Create a book of magazine clippings and photos you can print from the Internet that inspire you. Keep faith signs in front of you at all times.

NOTES:

#60
STOP VICTIM CONVERSATIONS

The Victim Vocabulary includes, "I don't have an education, I was abused as a child, and my parents chose divorce over me." Do not adopt this attitude. Fight it! Yesterday is over. Act like it. You have the anointing of God wrapped all around you. You are not a captive; you have been delivered. You are not a victim; you are a VICTOR"

"But you belong to God, my dear children. You have already won your fight...because the Spirit who lives in you is greater than the spirit who lives in the world"
I John 4:4 (NLT).

FAITH CHALLENGE:
Take 90 seconds and ask God to remind you of His victories in your life. Ask Him to help you remove all victim thoughts and conversations.

NOTES:

#61
LEARN SOMETHING NEW EVERYDAY

Wisdom is the ability to discern difference...in people, an environment, opportunities and moments. Wisdom comes from the Word of God. Solomon said that wisdom is the Miracle Key that unlocked life's house of treasure. Wisdom requires effort, time and persistence, but is worth the cost.

"Wisdom is supreme; therefore get wisdom. Though it costs all you have, get understanding"
Proverbs 4:7 (NIV).

FAITH CHALLENGE:
Take 90 seconds and ask God for wisdom in three key areas of your life (spiritual, work, family, purpose, finances, etc.).

NOTES:

#62
BUILD SOMEONE UP

A popular, but inaccurate statement is, "Words are cheap." Words cause wars. Words settle wars. Words create the waves of emotion that control our world. Your words of kindness today could easily create the wave that carries someone to his or her dreams.

"The tongue has the power of life and death, and those who love it will eat its fruit"
Proverbs 18:21 (NIV).

FAITH CHALLENGE:
Take 90 seconds and write down the name of three people who you can call, send a text or e-mail today with encouraging words to lift them up.

NOTES:

#63
HONOR EVERYONE'S OPINION

One of the greatest gifts you will ever give anyone is the gift of recognition. Every husband, wife and child is authorized by the Creator to have a point of view and an opportunity to express it. Honor their right to be heard. Something you need is often hidden in someone you may not enjoy. Listening is the seed that often produces favor.

"Do nothing out of selfish ambition or vain conceit, but in humility consider others better than yourselves"
Philippians 2:3 (NIV).

FAITH CHALLENGE:
Take 90 seconds and ask God to make you a committed listener to those He brings into your life today.

NOTES:

#64
PRACTICE CONFIDENTIALITY

Someone has said that even a fish wouldn't get caught if it kept its mouth shut. Confidentiality is a gift to be shared in the privacy of prayer or with a mentor God has assigned to your life. Never share your troubles with someone unqualified to help you. Silence cannot be misquoted.

"...discover not a secret to another: lest he that hears it put thee to shame, and thine infamy turn not away"
Proverbs 25:9-10 (KJV).

FAITH CHALLENGE:
Take 90 seconds and ask God to help you know when to use confidentiality. Remember only He is truly qualified to help you in any situation.

NOTES:

#65
TAKE A TINY STEP

Champions are those who are willing to move forward an inch at a time. Stay in movement today. Break down your goal into smaller steps. Progress creates joy. Two things are more important than your money, your energy and your time. Identify time wasters, those who diminish your energy, and limit their access to you. Small steps matter.

"Who despises the day of small things?"
Zechariah 4:10 (NIV).

FAITH CHALLENGE:
Take 90 seconds and list three small steps that you can take today to further reach your purpose and goal.

NOTES:

#66
POUR THE WORD
INTO YOUR MIND

Your mind gathers the dirt, grime and dust of human opinion everyday. Renew your mind to the Truth - God's Word. Schedule an appointment with the Bible daily. The renewing of your mind is the key to the changes within you. The Words of God are like waterfalls, washing and purifying your mind.

"And do not be conformed to this world, but be transformed by the renewing of your mind, that you may prove what is that good and acceptable and perfect will of God"
Romans 12:2 (NKJV).

FAITH CHALLENGE:
Take 90 seconds and memorize the scripture above. Now ask God throughout the day to renew your mind.

NOTES:

#67
IDENTIFY YOUR SUPPORT TEAM

Nobody succeeds alone. Nobody! Friends differ. Some correct you and others direct you. Some make you think and others make you feel. Identify those who truly stimulate you, educate you and empower you. Meticulously build your foundation for friendship, a support team that is a result of thought instead of convenience.

"Two are better than one, because they have a good return for their work: If one falls down, his friend can help him up. But pity the man who falls and has no one to help him up"
Ecclesiastes 4:9-10 (NIV).

FAITH CHALLENGE:
Take 90 seconds and write down the name of three friends who meet the above requirements. Now commit to giving each a call or email of appreciation in the next 24 hours.

NOTES:

#68
EXTRACT WISDOM FROM PROBLEMS

Examine problems for hidden wisdom. Learn how to make the best of every experience. When life sends you delays, think of it as extra time to read or catch up on correspondence. Think about all the potential advantages a problem might produce...exciting new challenges.

"Summing it all up, friends, I'd say you'll do best by filling your minds and meditating on things true, noble, reputable, authentic, compelling, gracious - the best, not the worst; the beautiful, not the ugly; things to praise, not things to curse"
Philippians 4:8 (The Message).

FAITH CHALLENGE:
Take 90 seconds and ask God what wisdom and potential advantages could come of your current challenges. Write these down and keep them in front of you.

NOTES:

#69
APPRAISE THE ATMOSPHERE

Native Americans would wet their fingers and hold them in the wind to discern the direction of air currents. You also must learn to observe and diagnose the currents, climate and emotional atmosphere others are creating around you. Their words are poison or power, doubt or faith. Their moods can be destructive or creative. Assess them accurately.

"When Jesus entered the ruler's house...he said, "Go away. The girl is not dead but asleep." But they laughed at him... he went in and took the girl by the hand, and she got up"
Matthew 9:23-25 (NIV).

FAITH CHALLENGE:
Take 90 seconds and ask God to help you discern the atmosphere around you and give you the courage to remove those destructive doubters.

NOTES:

#70
LINGER WITH THE LORD

Those who surround you influence what you become.
Something happens in the presence of God that doesn't happen anywhere else. Commands take a moment; plans take time.
Linger long enough to hear His plans.
Your views will change in His presence.
Your perceptions are corrected in His presence.
Your faith becomes focused in His presence.

*"You have made known to me the path of life;
you will fill me with joy in your presence,
with eternal pleasures at your right hand"
Psalms 16:11 (NIV).*

FAITH CHALLENGE:
Take more than 90 seconds and just be in His presence.

NOTES:

#71
CREATE YOUR FUTURE TODAY

A farmer sows his seeds months before he needs the harvest. Tomorrow is being decided right now. Your faith is moving into your future. Your investment in tomorrow is not lost. It simply goes into your future and begins to multiply.

"There's an opportune time to do things, a right time for everything on the earth: A right time for birth and another for death, A right time to plant and another to reap" Ecclesiastes 3:1-2 (The Message).

FAITH CHALLENGE:
Take 90 seconds and evaluate what kind of future you are creating for yourself. Are you investing in things that will multiply in your future (education, faith, ministry, etc.)? Commit to making the necessary adjustments today.

NOTES:

#72
DELETE VICTIM VOCABULARY

The Victim Vocabulary includes, "I was abused as a child, I don't have the right education," and
"My parent's divorce ruined my life."
DO NOT adopt this attitude! Fight it!
Yesterday is over. Act like it. You have the anointing of God wrapped around you. You are not a victim.
You are a victor.

"You, dear children, are from God and have overcome them, because the one who is in you is greater than the one who is in the world"
I John 4:4 (NIV).

FAITH CHALLENGE:
Take 90 seconds and ask God to help you remove any and all words from your vocabulary that do not correctly address who you are in His eyes.

NOTES:

#73
DO NOT FEED NEGATIVITY

There will be days when you are challenged to give place to bad attitudes. Someone will want to start an argument or gossip session. Do not permit it. Refuse to attend to a contentious spirit. It erodes your judgment and breaks your focus. Re-direct the conversation to the goodness of God and the potential of His blessings that are about to be birthed. Words decide futures.

"A gentle response defuses anger,
but a sharp tongue kindles a temper-fire"
Proverbs 15:1 (The Message).

FAITH CHALLENGE:
Take 90 seconds and ask God to help you be bold when challenged by negative attitudes.
Find scriptures that you can share to turn conversations.

NOTES:

#74
BECOME A BRIDGE

Someone may be ready to open up and share the dream of his or her heart with you. Listen.
Someone near you may long to hear an approving, encouraging word from you. Say it.
Someone may make a simple request that could unlock an important door for them. Do it.
You may be the only bridge to victory others ever experience.

"Love always protects, always trusts, always hopes, always perseveres"
I Corinthians 13:7 (NIV).

FAITH CHALLENGE:
Take 90 seconds and ask God to lead you to at least three people today. Then ask Him to give you the sensitivity to say what He would have you speak into their lives.

NOTES:

#75
CLOTHE YOUR MESSAGE PROPERLY

You are a walking billboard to others. Your appearance communicates an attitude toward the goals you are pursuing and the message you are sending. People see what you are before they hear what you are. Even Joseph dressed to create acceptance in the palace of Pharaoh.
Presentation is your gift to others.
It reveals what you consider most important.

"So Pharaoh sent for Joseph, and he was quickly brought from the dungeon. When he had shaved and changed his clothes, he came before Pharaoh"
Genesis 41:14 (NIV).

FAITH CHALLENGE:
Take 90 seconds and think about what your appearance is saying to others. You do not have to buy expensive clothing, but you do have to groom yourself, use great personal hygiene, and wear clean, well-kept clothing.

NOTES:

#76
SPRING CLEAN YOUR DREAMS

What excites you in your youth may bore you as you get older. Stop pursuing unexciting dreams. Be willing to relinquish previous goals that no longer stimulate you. Don't be a prisoner to the dreams of days gone by. Not finishing something you no longer desire does not make you a failure. Passion is a clue to a new season in your life. Energy is often a divine sign that you are on the right path.

"No, dear brothers and sisters, I am still not all I should be, but I am focusing all my energies on this one thing: Forgetting the past and looking forward to what lies ahead"
Philippians 3:13 (NLT).

FAITH CHALLENGE:
Take 90 seconds and "spring clean" your dreams. Decide right now to let go of pursuing things that no longer inspire you.

NOTES:

#77
MAKE GOD YOUR PARTNER

Let God decide your daily agenda and your dream will be achieved. A God-inspired dream will always require the participation of God. One hour with God could easily reveal that fatal flaws in your most carefully designed plans. If you succeed in prayer you will succeed. Have conversations with God just like you do your best friend. He responds to communication. Talking to God creates profound and indescribable results.

"It is not that we think we can do anything of lasting value by ourselves. Our only power and success come from God"
II Corinthians 3:5 (NLT).

FAITH CHALLENGE:
Take 90 seconds and commit absolutely everything in this day to the sovereignty of God. Give Him permission and complete control to guide your every step

NOTES:

#78
SOW YOURSELF

Sow a part of yourself into quality soil every day.
A seed is anything that you can say or do
that will benefit another person.
Your respect for others is a seed. Sow it.
Your knowledge shared is a seed. Sow it.
Your faith in others is a seed. Sow it.
Your love for others is a seed. sow it.
Your talent taught is a seed. Sow it.
What you make happen for others
God will make happen for you.

***"You know that the Lord will reward everyone
for whatever good he does"
Ephesians 6:8 (NIV).***

FAITH CHALLENGE:
Take 90 seconds and write down the names of three people
that you will sow into today. Do it with expectation.

NOTES:

#79
OPPOSITION PROVES PROGRESS

Warfare always surrounds the birth of a miracle. Nothing is ever as bad as it first appears. Battle is the opportunity to prove what you believe. Joseph proved that opposition is the road that takes you from the pit to the palace.
The size of your enemy determines the size of your reward. Do not let any enemy decide the timing of the battle nor the weapons you will use.

"In God I trust; I will not be afraid.
What can man do to me?"
Psalms 56:11 (NIV).

FAITH CHALLENGE
Take 90 seconds and remember the goal that is before you and how amazing it will feel when you have completed the task. Now let nothing stop you!

NOTES:

#80
CONFESS AND REMOVE SIN

Guilt is the thief of faith. When you permit sin in your life, you become uncomfortable in the presence of God. It is difficult to expect a miracle from the God you are at odds with.
Confess your failures. He forgives.
Confession is reaching. God always reacts to those reaching toward Him. Silence toward your own sin is arrogance. Seek the natural mercy that comes toward you. It came the moment you went to God for confession. The heaviest burden to carry in life is unconfessed sin.

"If I regard iniquity in my heart, the Lord will not hear me"
Psalms 66:18 (KJV).

FAITH CHALLENGE:
Take 90 seconds and go to God with humility in confession. Ask His forgiveness for all known sin. Then admit to Him that there are sins that you may not be aware of and that you need forgiveness for those as well. You will feel so much better.

NOTES:

#81
PURSUE YOUR MIRACLE

Pursuit is the proof of desire. You only reach for something that matters most. God has never responded to a need. He has never responded to tears. He only responds to faith.
The proof of faith is the willingness to reach.
ASK...reveals that you are a single question away from the solution.
SEEK...indicates that you must leave where you are, the place of comfort, to experience the answer.
KNOCKING...reveals that there is a door ready to be opened and a new dimension to be occupied.

""Keep on asking, and you will be given what you ask for. Keep on looking, and you will find. Keep on knocking, and the door will be opened. For everyone who asks, receives. Everyone who seeks, finds. And the door is opened to everyone who knocks"
Matthew 7:7-8 (NLT).

FAITH CHALLENGE:
Take 90 seconds and write down three questions to which you are willing to pursue the answer. Now approach God with faith and perseverance and He will respond.

NOTES:

#82
HOLD OUT FOR THE BEST

Hold fast to the promises God has given you. Don't be enticed into accepting less than God's very best for your life. Substitutes are common satanic ploys. Jesus was proof that God cared enough to send His very best. Your faith cannot respond to two targets. So, never consider any alternative to your miracle.

"But when you ask him, be sure that you really expect him to answer, for a doubtful mind is as unsettled as a wave of the sea that is driven and tossed by the wind. 7 People like that should not expect to receive anything from the Lord"
James 1:6-7 (NLT).

FAITH CHALLENGE:
Take 90 seconds and create a vivid photograph in your mind of the promise that God has given you. Make it clear and beautiful seeing God's very best as if it is already complete.
Hold this picture in your mind steadfast
until the day He brings it to pass.

NOTES:

#83
NEVER COMPLAIN ABOUT WHAT YOU PERMIT

Your circumstances are not permanent.
You have permitted your present circumstances or they would not exist. What you tolerate, you authorize to remain in your life. Either accept the present without complaint or make a decision to use your faith and attract a miracle from God.

"'If you can.'" said Jesus. 'Everything is possible for him who believes'"
Mark 9:23 (NIV).

FIATH CHALLENGE:
Take 90 seconds and decide what is in your life right now that you will no longer tolerate. Choose right now to stop complaining about things that you are not willing to address.

NOTES:_____

#84
SALVAGE A SOUL

You are not the only person who is struggling today. Others around you are hurting too. Be extremely attentive to the silent cries of someone close to you who may be drowning in an ocean of helplessness. One of the single best ways to begin feeling better about your current state
is to help someone who is in a worse state.

"Live creatively, friends. If someone falls into sin, forgivingly restore him..."
Galatians 6:1 (The Message).

FAITH CHALLENGE:
Take 90 seconds and ask God to bring you in contact with someone who is hurting. You could even schedule to spend time today (lunch hour or after work) to visit a senior care facility or homeless shelter.

NOTES:

#85
ANTICIPATE GOD

Your feelings are not your life.
Your worst circumstances today are not subject to change. God is stepping into the arena of your life. He is turning the tide of favor in your direction. You are never as far from a miracle as it first appears. The difference in seasons of your life is the God-instruction you are willing to follow.

"Every valley shall be raised up, every mountain and hill made low; the rough ground shall become level, the rugged places a plain. And the glory of the LORD will be revealed, and all mankind together will see it.
For the mouth of the LORD has spoken"
Isaiah 40:4-5 (NIV).

FAITH CHALLENGE:
Take 90 seconds and speak faith to God. Let Him know that you are not only ready but that you are expectantly looking for Him to show Himself in your life today.
God responds to faith!

NOTES:

#86
GO PROMOTE CHRIST

Promote the power of Jesus.
The first two letters of the word "Gospel" spell, "GO!"
Christianity is a network of activity. Promote Jesus today. He is the starting point of every miracle.
Be the bridge that connects Him to someone in trouble today.
Be bold. One miracle is worth a thousand sermons.

"He said to them, 'Go into all the world and preach the good news to all creation'"
Mark 16:15 (NIV).

FAITH CHALLENGE:
Take 90 seconds and create a Facebook post, an email or a text to promote Jesus. Ask God to bring you in contact with a hungry soul and to give you miracle words to speak into their lives.

NOTES:

#87
HONOR THE LAW OF SOWING AND REAPING

The Scriptural law of sowing and reaping is universal. Fools deny it. Rebels defy it. The wise live by it. When you sow love, you will reap love. Inventory your seeds of time, mercy, honor and finances. Lavishly sow into quality soil.
Harvest is inevitable.

"Don't be misled. Remember that you can't ignore God and get away with it. You will always reap what you sow"
Galatians 6:7 (NLT).

FAITH CHALLENGE:
Take 90 seconds and choose three seeds that you will sow today (time, mercy, honor, talent, resources, finances, love, etc.). Now commit to sowing them abundantly.

NOTES:

#88
GIVE YOUR WAY OUT OF TROUBLE

Your seed is always a bridge out of trouble. The widow of Zarephath used her seed to create a harvest in the middle of a great famine. Something in your possession is the key to your future. What God has already placed in your life is always enough to get you out of trouble. However, it will do you no good in the barn. Get it planted.

"Do not neglect your gift, which was given you through a prophetic message when the body of elders laid their hands on you"
I Timothy 4:14 (NIV).

FAITH CHALLENGE:
Take 90 seconds and ask God to reveal the seed and the soil you can use to build a bridge from where you are into your favored future.

NOTES:

#89
BECOME SOMEONE'S HARVEST

You are a seed.
Sow yourself into the future.
Sow yourself into someone else.
You are an investment into the divine destiny
that God has for someone near you.
See yourself as the blessing others are looking for.
He is the Blessor; you are the Blessing.

*"Give away your life; you'll find life given back, but not merely given back - given back with bonus and blessing. Giving, not getting, is the way.
Generosity begets generosity"
Luke 6:38 (The Message).*

FAITH CHALLENGE:
Take 90 seconds and create a list of blessings you could be for someone else. Now ask God to reveal at least three people for whom you can become a harvest.

NOTES:

1) A good friend & a Mentor
2) A financial Blessing
3) Provide a ride for someone w/out a car.

#90
CREATE YOUR FUTURE

You will never leave where you are, until you decide where you want to be. The day you make a decision about life is the day your world will change. Move decisively toward the goals you have established. Partner with a mentor or coach who will work beside you to create your future.

"Forget the former things; do not dwell on the past. See, I am doing a new thing! Now it springs up; do you not perceive it? I am making a way in the desert and streams in the wasteland"
Isaiah 43:18-19 (NIV).

FAITH CHALLENGE:
Take 90 seconds and visit my website:
(www.NathanFaught.com)
Let me partner with you to discover
and fulfill God's plan for your life.

NOTES:

PROLOGUE

Congratulations. You made it!

What an amazing accomplishment. I pray that the last 90 days have brought you to a place where your faith is stronger, more real and effective than you have ever experienced.

These last 90 days were not meant to be a journey in and of themselves as much as a beginning to a brand new faith journey that will grow through the rest of your days.

The individual who begins a new exercise regimen and has seen positive results, must continue their routines and even challenge themselves further so they may continue to grow. In the same way, you too must continue to exercise your faith and find new challenges for it to grow.

May God continue to richly bless you as your faith journey brings you closer and closer to Him.

- *Nathan Faught*

As a thank you for taking "THE CHALLENGE"
I would like to offer you
a **_FREE_** coaching session.
Visit www.nathanfaught.com today
and follow the link
"Free Coaching Session"

Nathan Faught
1019 N Faulkner Dr
Claremore, OK 74017
www.nathanfaught.com

Made in the USA
Charleston, SC
13 March 2013